Come
Cold River

For Marina

Here is the river
we all swim in—
Karen

Come
Cold River

Karen Connelly

QUATTRO BOOKS

The publication of *Come Cold River* has been generously supported by the Canada Council for the Arts and the Ontario Arts Council.

Author's photograph: Anne Bayin
Cover image: Anne Bayin
Cover design: Sarah Beaudin
Editor: Allan Briesmaster
Typography: Grey Wolf Typography

Library and Archives Canada Cataloguing in Publication

Connelly, Karen
        Come cold river / Karen Connelly.

Poems.
ISBN 978-1-927443-47-7 (pbk.)

        I. Title.

PS8555.O546C66 2013   C811'.54   C2013-904273-3

Published by Quattro Books Inc.
Toronto, ON
info@quattrobooks.ca
www.quattrobooks.ca

Printed in Canada

For the women
forgotten, remembered.

For Lucas and Jasmin, beloved.

If the water, everywhere, and if she
is. If ghosts, like water, like if all
rivers and oceans and rains are one
ghost, surrounding and throughout . . .
If she is . . .
If she is the sound, if it isn't
essential until its lack. If she is
the sound of. Waves. If in the body,
the dew in morning, and the moon.
If she is the sound of the water.
If rising, if breaking, if throughout.

—CJ Evans, "Elegy in Limestone"

Contents

Home for Good

On maps of the territories that would eventually become Canada, Spanish explorers sometimes wrote *Acá Nada*, which translates into 'There, nothing'. This is a possible origin for the country's name. *Kanata* is also a word in St. Lawrence Iroquoian. Meaning village or settlement, it is the most commonly cited etymological origin for 'Canada'.

The name of my country is the word of an ancient (and living) nation. Or it is nothing.

To think, haltingly, confusedly, about this fact means that I have to look back at my early childhood, which was marked by various losses. But it was also marked by Cree, T'suu T'ina, and Siksika words and places. Every single day, they were there in my life: home, river, ponds, fields, asphalt streets. All were haunted. And I loved them.

Forget. Forgot. Forgotten.

Then the season changed: another light, a new time.

And I began to remember.

why the poem?

the poem
is alone in the forest

another goddamn pervert
whetting his steel blade
against granite

can you hear the steady
shk shhk shhk shhhhk shhhhhhk

the poem is the down
that sweetens the hen's bony neck

it is the old wood
crying out in a parched voice
burn me
burn me

here is the poem, sparks leaping
like a swirl of scarlet water
into fire

and here, it is
the ashes
the ashes

why the poem?
because no one will hear it

amongst the blabbers at the table
this voice falls
silent

small speechless tree in the forest

who
who
snow-winged owl, the poem lifts
      rises into this night of words

Home for Good

With burning hearts we see the rise
in the price of the old neighbourhood
by the river where my mom
played as a kid, grew up, married
the wrong man, a crook,
then to increase her mistake exponentially
and complicate my family tree,
left him and married his brother.
Daddy, Daddy!
He was more hardworking than the other
but equally ruinous.

It's too damn bad she didn't keep the house.
It would be worth half a million now.

True north, strong, no longer free
for the taking. No wonder
we have to stand on guard
in this town. Where there's money
there's a lack of it, and thieves.

Who believes that Divino's Bar
once was a little place, bohemian yet elegant.
Today it's buffed new and polished blunt.
The light fixture cost fifty thou
and the wine list starts off
—don't ask me how—
at three hundred a bottle.

But I used to nurse a teabag there
for hours, without shame
across from a red-haired Englishman
who taught me how to touch the flame
that burns sapphire-blue above Sambucca.

Ah. The first time, my very first
to see a floating coffee bean
and quench my thirst
with fire. Alcohol, at last.

Now I can't afford to be
nostalgic by the glass.

Perhaps (the ghost of my uncle quips)
I should take out a quick loan
and rip off a liquor store on my own
or play the VLT's (that's for Video Lottery Terminals)
until the cows
come
home
Just take a chance!

Like my dad
who gave my inheritance
toonie by toonie to the AGLC
(that's for Alberta Gaming and Liquor Commission).

No complaints from me
though I wish on
my mother's grave
that some of my father's cash
could splash down helter-skelter
into a food bank stash
or a women's shelter.
Both proclaim their desperate need
despite tons of oil and cattle feed.

From far and wide, oh Canada
and Calgary too,
I have loved you
desperately
and departed.

I can't remember
—can you remember?—
how this song started.

And how does it end?
Am I home for good
or for bad? Home to stay
and bury the hatchet
or dig it up
and throw it?

Here, catch it
in your scarred hands
catch it in that rotting treasure
your tarred and feathered oil sands
catch it nimbly
between your teeth.
It's that trick
with an axe
you taught me.

Acá nada. Kanata.
Oh Canada, what do you *really* mean?
How can I sing you
without lying?

Familiar

i.

I walked through Wetaskiwin
Medicine Hat   Red Deer
camped in the Kananaskis
stared into the opal light
of Minnewanka.

Indian names
my mother explained, *Indian lands.*
Sitting in the backyard
drinking a beer, she flicked her eyes
over the poplars, the bird bath,
the small plastic swimming pool,
and said, *They lived here*
before we did. This was all
theirs.

Sometimes I rode a horse
from the stables
along the Tsuu T'ina Reserve.
I saw the trees but I never saw a Tsuu T'ina.

Or did I?

ii.

Indian was the only word
we used back then, confused as ever
about the continent,
the shipwreck,
our wreckage.

The only Indian at school
was Ryan, bigger than the other kids,
merciless grabber of girls' breasts and thighs.

Attraction is recognition.
When his curses leapt off the brick walls
I caught them in my mouth.

One day, after a fight, I screamed
        Ryan, kiss my ass!
He came loping across the field yelling,
        I'd love to kiss your stupid white ass.
        Just give it to me!
I bolted for home like a hungry pony.

The next day we sparred
again in the playground.
I shrieked laughter
ran away, returned
could not find him.

I asked the teacher,
Where did Ryan go?
She would not say
where, or how, who took him.

Prison, I thought. And my fault.
I had told on him once.
After he pinched my new breast.
Mr. Schmidt said, "That's just what boys do."

They must have sent him to jail
because he was as tall as a man
and swore like one, too.
I'm FBI, Ryan told me.
That's Fucking Big Indian.

Would he ever escape?
Maybe. I hoped for and
feared it. He might be
                mad at me, ten-year-old author
                of his fate. Once I had wished him
                gone. Now I missed him, my giant
                familiar.

iii.

Home and native land,
                how can I know you?

You do not belong to me.

A woman with a rusted key
under my tongue
                how can I belong to you?

I dream outside your wild mouth.
Upon waking, I yearn for another country
                but I was born here.

        How did I get lost
                with this map in my hand?

        Teach me again, grasshopper field,
                to lie down with the sky.

        River I knew before words,
                sing me.

        Return, old cottonwood of the child's mind
                and you, little rock
                        small grey rock in my pocket
                                whisper the way

to the Weaselhead paths
        I wandered as a girl
                praying for frogs

and found
        one, once, in the pond mud
            its throat rounded out,
                translucent with song.

Sun heavy as a horse's head
        leaning long hot bones
            along my back
    I crouched to watch
        the amphibian skin stretch
            balloon   not break.

I listened to that single proclamation
    ours ours ours

and remembered Ryan
        stolen, like the language he would have spoken
  Tsuut'ina
        great great grandson of Chief David Crowchild
            bronc-rider, builder of roads
              and houses, bearer
                of shelter.

But Ryan grew unhoused.

Was he there in the poplars?
Cursing spitting aspen spirit
    and laughing.
        Could he see me?

My feet sank into the mud
    as Frog's throat filled again
        and gold-stippled eyes stared
            through the skating whirling lives
                of water.

When I opened my mouth

    he dove
        through me

                into lime-green algae
                leapt free into the hidden country.

The War

For my sister Tracy Kochis. In memoriam.

I did not carry a gun.

There were guns in the house
but I was a civilian, a child.
I knew we were all going to die

but I did not.

I knew
about torture
because I was there.
I watched the naked girl
screaming
into the twisted sheet
as the man beat the truth
out of her with a piece of wood.
What was the truth?
The truth was her life.

To see was a crime
against him, to not see.
was a crime against her.
I loved them equally,
the destroyer, the destroyed.
They were mine, inside me,
that girl, that man.

Because I could not look away
I was severed
by the guillotine of light
dropping through the slit
between the door frame
and the slightly-open door,

the child cut in half
by the every-day war
and the beloved hands that waged it,
the sister twisting on the bed,
the father
beating the life out of her,
out of himself.

My sister used to hitchhike all the time

She was the woman
                walking on the edge
                of the highway
        so small compared
                to the road stretching
                        over the distant hill
                                her white chest pressed
                                against the black sky.

I was that woman, too, the one
        who walks into the roar of the wind
        at 2 a.m., her face turned away from the gale
                while her eyes stare directly into it.

She is the woman
        who is wrong, who lies, who strides
                into the tunnel of her drunken mind
                and stumbles out the other side
                        into the common despair of morning.

I am still that woman,
                fucked over and under and inside out
                        and I am too tired to care anymore
                                because home is so far away
                                I will never get there.

She is the woman
        who loves the storm when it comes
                even as it soaks her jean jacket and shoes
                and her socks become grey rags.

My hair is stuck to my scalp and chin,
        makeup runs down my face,
            I am so damn cold
                and crying, trying,
                trying to find
                        that word, the right word,
                        the one I always lose.

The woman is sick
        of the cars thrashing her spirit
            as they speed by, oblivious.
She knows the one that finally stops
                is driven by a man
                who can hurt her.

The truck skidding over to the shoulder of the road
            is Death asking a blunt question.

        He pushes open the door.

                Sometimes she answers by getting inside.
                Sometimes she answers by walking on.
                Often he answers for her.

The Truth

If I found the truth there
I found it in alleys, edges, tracks
where the city split open
and weeds slipped in, green knives.
The truth I befriended
did not walk out
with the honest people,
or open in the smiling faces
on the steps of the good houses.
Though the houses *were* good,
the truth should have chosen to live in them.

But it did not.
No, it was obstinate, rude,
the worst sort of junkie. Belligerent.
The truth once said, "I shall set you free."
But it was joking.
The truth kept itself to itself
in an apartment building blackened
by weather everyone denied.
That's always where the truth resides.

I walked past it as I always had,
I saw, I could not see it, I carried it in my hands
like a weapon I didn't know how to use.
The truth was there next to me like a lover
but as usual I was afraid
of commitment because
I was only thirteen.

Later, I was surprised
by the splintered door,
the cries. Then darkness
growing like placenta
around me, the first and last
force of blood.

The Breakfast Cereal of His Youth

For David, wherever breakfast finds him

Why, I asked, is it called crack?

Because, my brother began, a smile on his face
like the smirk of a scientist
explaining the solar system
to a peasant

because it crackles when you cook it
up and suck it in
snap–crackle–pop
the smoke swirls,
the pipe's so hot
you burn your mouth
(the hotter the higher the faster)

because it gives you cracked lips

because if you smoke too much
it smashes your heart to smithereens.

Because it breaks your life
into before
and after
the first inhalation
when every complication falls away.
It takes ten seconds for the pleasure-flood
of dopamine to drown the brain.
Flood of no return.
The ship splinters open
spills the little white rocks.

Again the patronizing smile.
How handsome he is, silk boy
amongst gangsters. Smooth.

When he speaks he is half-devil
and pure hunger.
It's still years before the years
in prison whittle down his face.

Give me this, he said
          (fourteen years old, how could he know
                    what he was asking for?)
Give me this
          (as children we heard that request night after night)
Give me this
          (bottle clank, chime of ice, blood on Dad's shirt
                    after a fight)

          (Do you remember
            the sallow light of his room
            early morning or dusk
            the white shirt on the floor stained brown
            noose of cigarette smoke swinging in the air
            the rest of the house a long way off)

It will kill you, I tell him.
He shrugs.
Snap crackle pop.
Black eyes turn and lock
into mine
like a gun ready to use.

The barrel
shoots backward.

          Can you take this

                    the creosote rush

                    the coming roar

A Good Question

He always mentioned
the Alfa Romeo to the new girls
though he preferred
to fuck us in his SUV.

More room.
Murderers like them, too,
more space to hold a woman
down and move her carcass around
even if she's not a crack whore.

A cop told me that, actually.

Working, you have your own
death in your mind.
That's why I carry a knife.
And I know how to use it.

Anyway, for sex he takes
us to a deserted stretch in Ogden
or all the way out of town.
The girl can give him head while he drives.
He likes to listen to music to get in the mood.
Emma said he loved ABBA.
That really wrecked "Mamma Mia" for me.

Emma, what a rich kid's name.
And she was.
A lawyer's daughter.
Strathcona, the private school, riding lessons,
the works. But. At parties, her dad liked to give her
to his clients. She was the goody bag.

Out they go, towards Okotoks this time.
When Romeo's done, she hops out of the car
to take a pee beside the highway

not wearing her shoes of course.

Maybe it wouldn't have mattered
if she *had* been wearing them.
They were stilettos.
How far can you walk in those?
It's just the idea, you know.

Emma is squatting *ahhhhh*
when he starts
the car.
Spinning tires
spit gravel
at her thighs.

                    Hey, what the fuck?
                    Where ya goin'?

The car pulls around
loops back onto the highway
aimed like a dick into Calgary.

Which is exactly where the fucker went
left her standing there
no shoes
no underwear under her skirt.

The guy drives an Alfa Romeo
and he rips off her shoes and her purse
her whole take for the night.

She has to walk back to Calgary
barefoot after midnight
scared shitless
that someone sicker
than the prick who left her there
is going to stop and pick her up.

Only guys from the reserve
and women with a death wish
hitchhike that late at night.

By the time she gets close enough
to catch a bus,
her feet bleed a lot on the floor.
The driver is decent enough to give her a free ride.

When she gets back downtown
and calls me, she's howling like a baby.
I take her to emergency myself
in Grandma's old Bronco.

It's a good truck. Rusted out piece
of shit but valiant, you know?
A real truck, not a stupid SUV.

We smoke up in the hospital
parking lot before going inside.
Hours later, she howls again
because the nurse has to open
every cut and clean it out.
She asks Emma

                    What happened here?
                    Did someone torture you?

Her eyes go dry. She winces a smile.
That's a good question, she replies.

Dinner Time

For Ken, wherever dinner time finds him

We ate the bird you killed.
You looked away from the tiny dinosaur eye,
already extinct, and slit her throat
with a grace I didn't recognize.
It made me wonder who you were
before I existed.

Cinnamon-limbed, thin.
Gripping his mother's thigh
in Detroit, circa 1966. Hazel eyes halt
at every train station, ransack the continent.
A boy abandoned
by one father then exposed
to another, as some children
are exposed to lead.
Or the elements.

When the other siblings grew soft
and died or fled, you stayed,
turned hard, harder.
You grew nails, hammers,
brick, mortar, up at five,
you showered as he drank
his coffee, closed the door.
How old were you?
Fifteen. Sixteen.
No money for boots,
you wore old running shoes
into the winter mornings,
apprentice brick-layer, a man
who earned his living
with his hands, skin, muscle,
each gold nugget in his bent spine,
spent

when two weeks before
you had been a teenage boy
who painted the sun drinking the ocean
with a straw, a kid who grasped instinctively
the rules of perspective.
Truck driver's son, you knew
how to pronounce
chiaroscuro correctly

but needed other words,
heavier tools, shovels, picks,
saws, plumblines, fists.

I remember the two of you together.
That fight at dinner time, table upturned,
glass shattered against the wall, the little ones
howling: he would murder you.
Irritation came later: he didn't.

Hungry, territorial, you fought
me furiously for bread, for meat.
For air. And always won.
Oh, finger-bending bully,
my brother. So close.
Foreign. Adopted
from that old warrior kingdom.
We could not understand
each other's language.

Yet when you killed the hen,
I grasped the lexicon as easily
as you held the knife.
Slaughter is a pure act
of life. When you fed me
I thought of our father
tirelessly skinning the deer
that hung from the rafters.

Their severed forelegs
became your favourite backyard weapons,
gleaming obsidian hoof at one end,
red-flecked white bone at the other.

But no one killed anyone
in our family or even drew blood
that often. That's what you said:
It's not such a big deal.

After the meal, you led me
into the dark outside.
Moon shorn of her face,
drowned stars,
pond a lacquered hole.

The trees around us stood
invisible, pulsing like arteries
inside the sealed night of the human.
You laughed at your sister from the city,
hesitating on a road she could not see.
You told me where to put my feet.

Later, we drove through rape seed, wheat,
into the voracious glow of Calgary,
each of us thinking silently
of the boy,
that feast.

Knot

Tight knot
of rope, it lashed
the boy to the mast
that brought the ship
through storms, the bow
plunging
down the waves,
heaving
toward a sky
no one
could see.

In the fairytale
in the newspaper
in the courtroom
they said
the boy offered himself up.

It was not punishment.
He chose it
the mast
the keelhauling the rope
the knot the knot
he cannot undo it,
cannot find the *no*
at the centre
of the word,
at the core
of the child
who tied himself
to salted lightning
storm water
filling his mouth.

Was he a sewer
to take it
in?
Or a lightning rod
to be struck?

After the storm, the crew explained
it was not intended
it was a mistake
it was the destruction
wrought by the violent weather
of those times
and the captain
was no wise man.
What else could he make
of his son?

Tie me
the child said
to the mast
and I will watch
the raging sea.

I will lead us through
the troughs
the swells
the valley of the shadow.

Rocks?
I will see them.

A safe shore?
I will become it.

A shipwreck?
I will take it
in my throat.

Crow

crack-crack
taps the crow
with the shell
on the rock

laughing bird
black glister on grey dirt

warbles and clicks
in the blue-black throat

snap and swipe
of the beak

so sharp
head cocks
eye hooks you live

hop hop
and caw
calling the river

crack-crack
against the egg-smooth rocks
head shake

swipe-swipe
open

Little One

Vancouver, January, 2002

Hour of return
3:07 a.m.

Thirty years later,
she swims back.

Three years old
in the bathroom

realm of white tile
waste

the only door
with a lock

the toddler
and her father
inside.

Outside, fog.

Water drops from the eaves,
beads off trees.
The waves creep up the shore.

Beyond the black hole
and the dwarf star
face the first warp

that weft of light
under the door

The welter of our time

Oh, alien meteor

Missing pieces

Ashes ashes
all fall down

The girl, the father, the water.

A trinity?

Or a baptism?

No. It was a miracle.

He drowned her,
he resurrected her.

She was clean at the end of it.
Rosy. Bathed.

In the bathroom she stares
into the mirror
at her halved face

one eye a black hole
one eye unscathed

Begin the familiar interrogation.

    Are you making this up?
It was so long ago,
are you sure?
I know
what a good
liar you are girl.

    How can I trust you now?

Where are
    what is
        missing?

        a piece
            of tape in the brain

            memory tape

            duct tape, she is

            a piece of

       the pieces   the pieces

         ashes ashes all

           who

           who

The same question, time after time.
It has become a cliché. Or bad joke.
Embarrassment.

Please don't tell it again.
No one wants to hear it.

Go on then.
Dry your hair, little one.
Hop into bed.
Turn off the light.
Stop crying.
Time to sleep.

But I can't.
I can't sleep.

Night after night, I lie
suspended inside trapezoids
of streetlight
                headlights
   darklight.

Shadows plunge
       across the ceiling
              like figures pointing
                   from the gunwales of a boat.

Is she down there?

Can you find her?

I am a small blue crab
enamoured of the sand
beholden to the current
that lifts and casts
its gritty net of silica

I scrabble through
the glassy ripple
sideways

Humans at the surface
windmill fleshy arms
through distant air

I pick the scabby
treasure chest

Quick, little one
scuttle into the lock

claws tap-tap
tap-tap
and twist back

What do I see
underground
underskin

what is here
glinting
in mirrors
of sand?

Swim back

through the cave
into the mouth
of the heart

find the treasure chest
under sand and sea
that pit of memory

open it

out

      floats the child

            seaweed for hair
            fish scale skin
            flippered tail

after so many years
down here
she knows how
to breathe
water

Now she flips over
in a moment bares
her human eyes

now
　　her hand
　　　　wavers, rippling

　　　her hand
　　　　　reaches
　　　　　　for your hand

Enough

In February, 2002, the RCMP began to excavate the Pickton farm in Port Coquitlam, B.C. The 68 women commemorated in this poem disappeared during the years that Robert Pickton was killing his victims; he was charged with the murders of 26 of them. Despite years of racist negligence and incompetence, no law enforcement agency or officer was ever held accountable for failing to protect Vancouver's vulnerable women.

Each night I walk
into the ocean
and drown again.

Marie Laliberté

Each morning I read
the newspaper,
watch the CBC.

Ruby Hardy

Hands hang limp
and empty off my knees.

Angela Rebecca Gardine

I am a creature
trapped in the net

Teresa Triff

of every rainy morning,
snared in the little word
evil.

Andrea Faye Borhaven

What is severed?
Head of the animal, or the tail?
My mouth opens.

Cara Ellis

Closes.
Eyes burn and swivel
above the jammed throat.

Ingrid Soet

Do you dare
speak?
What word?

Heather Kathleen Bottomley
Jennifer Lynn Furminger
Jacqueline McDonell
Sereena Abotsway
Kerri Lynn Koski
Mona Wilson
Andrea Joesbury
Diana Melnick
Sharon Abraham
Angela Arsenault
Georgina Faith Papin

Finally there are enough
dead women
to begin.

Cops visit the farm
with a search party.

Bones.
Blood-stained blouse.
Asthma inhaler.
Halved skulls.

Let's start the familiar interrogation.

Was she making it up, Officer,
her own disappearance?

Now she lies
—it's true—
beneath you.

How do you like it?
Here?
Mmm. Or right
there?

You are stepping on her knuckle now.
Soon, her blood-caked hair.

Let's watch the dig.

Our bulldozers.
Our forensic tents
slackened by rain.
Our brave men.
They appear on cue
with coffee, keen dogs.

Our own torture chamber.
And that's just one of our national
killing floors. There are more.
Here is the conveyor belt
of debris (eyes hearts teeth).
Dozens of chains
of DNA. Unlinked.
Unlinked. Unlinked.

Yes, a lot of the girls
were Native. We try
not to discriminate
except when it comes
to this. To them.

Unfold the maps on the table.
Let me show you hell.
As described in *The Globe and Mail.*
It includes English Bay,
blue salt water, sand, crows,
owls in the cedars.

The road out?
Oh, that remains
under construction.

I save the articles, the photographs.
Tape them to my bedroom wall.

Helen Mae Hallmark

The women stare into me.
They ask. They ask.

Dawn Teresa Crey

On my knees on the floor
in the middle of this room
at the edge of the country

Janet Henry

I await

Julie Young

a single word.

Sherry Leigh Irving

Seven names.

Patricia Rose Johnson

Twelve faces one week.

Cindy Beck

Twenty the next.

Cynthia Feliks

Any word

Sarah de Vries

The word

Rebecca Guno

For. Against.

Tiffany Louise Drew

Thirty throats

We cried out for you

Forty

Fifty sisters

Sixty eight

girls

Sixty eight women

mothers

Sixty eight daughters.

Officers,
you started
your party
too late.

Marcella Creison

Elsie Sebastian

Heather Gabrielle Chinnock

Angela Arsenault

Olivia William

Brenda Anne Wolfe

Dorothy Spence

Aging newspaper between the fingers.
Blurred words. Beaten pulp
of the tree's heart.

Nancy Clark

See how quickly

Kellie Little

a woman

Laura Mah

disappears

Debra Lynne Jones

under wet hooves

Frances Young

under police reports

Leigh Miner

lost

Mary Ann Clark
Inga Monique Hall

misfiled

Marnie Lee Frey
Tanya Marlo Holyk
Dianne Rosemary Rock
Sheryl Donahue

and ignored.

Yvonne Teresa Boen
Sharon Ward
Wendy Crawford
Sheila Egan
Catherine Knight
Marie Abigosis

Yes. The pigs.

The country's clean white teeth
crunch crunch
grind the matter
back into the manageable dirt
of everyday.

Our headlines.
Our chatter.

I touch the faces

Catherine Gonzalez
Sherry Baker

photographs of the faces

Taressa Williams
Elaine Allenbach

Let me out   Let me out

of this narrow frame

Her fingers slide
through the clouded mirror

Michelle Gurney

Eyes and mouth

Elaine Dumba

bloom in the silver aperture
resolve into shoulder

breasts
warm ribcage
legs running
rivulets of clean water

Stephanie Lane
Tania Petersen
Sherry Rail

Wish me
walking back

stepping away
from his truck

Kathleen Wattley
Jacqueline Murdock

Wish me another road

the well-lit side

Wish me hot tea
in the van with Bonnie

Gloria Fedyshyn
Lillian O'Dare

Wish me
the promise word
song word
vow
       my mother's name
       my child's name

Wish me
the earth rolling over
       to unlatch the window
            of dawn.

Wish me through.

Jane Doe

Awake

Command

In the heart of the field
a chair stands astonished
by September twilight.
Over the headland, the edge
of Turkey spreads violet,
split amethyst in God's hand.

But what if I cannot believe?

The bones
of the hills begin
to fade into the trees.
Valley: thighs of a woman sliding
perpetually into her azure bath.
The sky sinks into the sea, the sea
into the valley, the valley disappears.

Sudden dark.
Only the lights of the village glint
and tremble, rough basket of stars.

What if, when the morning comes,
it does not finish the night
but magnifies it, like the fairytale
I heard as a child –
only shorn of its ending,
the bliss.

What if the kiss
doesn't wake me?

*

Before the shepherd arrives at dawn
I trace the perimeter of the field
        purple thistle   oregano
        wind-hiss   stone wall
            fallen down.

The olive trees. Solitude.
Trying to walk to the end of it
but unable.

I do up the buttons on my shirt
like the rest of them.

I take my place
in the dumb careening flock
and greet the disaster every day.

I love this warm red stone
whispering in my hand.

*

Not a kiss
but a command.
The blue chair
upright among the olives
orders me to *Sit!*
Like a hungry dog,
I obey.

Pledged to rose petals
in dust, I sit.
And I stay.
I stay.

The Lost Father

From the beginning I sensed
        we were not alone.
We opened the tall windows
        to the walnut trees, the sea.
The length of his body
        was a sail bearing me far
        into my body.

The room was empty with newness,
        walls gypsum-white,
                sheets chalk-white,
                corners keen and bright with echo.
But we were not alone.

His whispers came urgently
        from the edge of the narrow bed.
He was like a child at prayer.
His father had died the year before.
The salt rasped in his throat
        but he could not cry.
For a year, he had not touched, not opened.

Now death pushed through him
and flooded the room.
I adored my father.

When he whispered these words,
        I felt awe before the miracle
        of the good man
                who left love in his wake
                        like phosphorescence, the father
                                worth the cut and shine of tears.

Not knowing who to mourn for, I dove into the ocean
        of flesh, clutching my own
                need like a net
                        so much caught
                        so much spilling through.

The steady waves pounded through us.
Naked swimmers, we searched
        sounded the depths   dove under
                kicked down a fathom
                        deeper and found him finally

                        the lost father

                        we found him

                                and hauled the ruined
                                human body
                                up into the light.

Symadia

i.

Given signs,
you took them.
The naked woman
behind the glass wall
spread her cunt open
with her fingers.
When you saw the tiny diamond
piercing the oyster lip,
lust split open in your gut.
The woman touched
herself for your pleasure,
you took it, the woman
leaned against the white horse,
glanced over her shoulder
at your camera, arched
her back to show you
the bronze curve of her ass,
slit and glitter, the sign
at the crossroads where
you took her left, right,
plunged into the crux

while she remained standing
behind the glass of herself
and you lay trapped
in your eyes, hands
filled with sweat-slick flesh,
empty, your body drifting away,
a spent man sinking in the nameless sea.

ii.

Signs.
You could do nothing
but take them.

The beach at Naxos was impossible
to find that first day.
You searched fields of thorn and wire
between white villages, hot skin
of sky, salt-dust on your face.
The Aegean looped around you,
dancing at a distance, singing,
but no road to approach her.

An old woman in a black dress told you.
A young woman in a white dress told you.
A woman named the path through fields of stone,
the way to find that water.

The beach at Naxos.
Mother of blue, sister in silver.
The sand dunes rose and fell
like another naked body, many bodies.
You stepped into them, walked through them,
sun glinting off silica, burning sand under your feet,
grit on your scalp, glass unmade and salt dried white
down the length of your body, the sign to look back.

When you turned: footprints.
A child's feet. But you could not see him.
He whispered to you, *anemos*,
the wind. You could not see him.

Autumn thrust you again to Athens.
Among so many papers, crucial meetings,
Omonia and her market of women at three in the morning,
money rising up like the buildings of your name,
there was now a haunting,
not a ghost but the boy,
walking where you walked, a breath distant,
a breath close, what was it, he asked you,
what was it, your name?

Where was the wind but over the sea?
You glimpsed your name above
the gleaming backs of the dolphins,
their fins heaving like ploughs
in blue and silver soil.

After signs, you sailed back to Naxos.
Symadia for twenty years. Odysseus
searching for home in his flesh.

iii.

Signs.
But here there is no taking.
The islands give themselves to you.

You dream of a goddess
washing her hair.
When the drops fall, spray
of diamonds, islands
are born of the sea.
Naxos. Amorgos. Mykonos.
Ios. Santorini. Milos. Water
encircling each
and the dolphins splicing
between the waves

like blade-shaped cells,
the first shining sons
and daughters.

In the sweet haul of light
before dawn, you hear a woman calling
and rush down to the sea.
The child plays near her wet feet.

You walk toward him, finally.
You can do nothing else.
He smiles up at you
and sings your name.

I Awake

I awake to him
holding my forearm
the way a child holds the neck
of the horse after the reins
have slipped past the tangled mane.
The mare gallops, gallops.

Hours before, the hooves
of sex pounded high, hard
inside our throats,
sweat-sleek skin
hot with fear flipped over
into love made matter,
voiced, *Will you run me down?*

Yes. Trampled. The silver-green trees blurred
above two bodies rushing into light.

Now we are still.
The only movement, breath.
I lie here with his hands
holding me as I run
nowhere.
Then slowly turn
my head to see the stars
beyond the grapevine
at the window's edge.
Heart of my heart, that vine
was planted before I was born.

I leave him to see the stars better.
And hear him breathing
inside the small house
as I always heard him breathing

but did not listen
with the clear faith
of water.

Now that I am drowned
and risen again, I know.
Now I know.
When the man shifts in bed,
I listen.

I listen without sorrow, as the nightingales
sing without it.
If there is a broken note
in their song, it is we
who have broken it.

Sheep bells ring in the field:
water falling on stone, striking copper.
The birds serenade the dark.
My feet grow cold
beneath the stars.

Another moment here
in the cricketing
glittering silence,
then beside him
I will lie down,
slowly,
touch his forearm
and sleep.

The Children

I feel them falling
out of me,
the children,
like the passage
of stars in the sky,
the small fire denied
by the fierce rising
of the sun, the burning
of my own life.

They turn their small hands
up to me sadly, they don't know
how to cry because
they haven't been born,
but they regret even that, the pain
of the life I refuse them.
Nothing deters these ones:
not this great slaughterhouse
Earth, not the bad genetics,
not even sullen poverty.

It is a miracle,
how willing they are
to live.

I think it is because
they do not believe
they will have to die.
Or, being so small, so immense,
they cannot fathom death.
They regard the newspaper
without fear.
They curiously observe
the sobbing.

They come to the door
at dawn when the crow is passing
and in their veined, translucent palms
they hold the shadows of their own
bones and teeth.

They whisper, *Please*
then glare up at me,
pouting. Inconsolable.
Faux-tragique.
When I turn away in disgust,
they laugh like foxes.
I recognize them.
Their voices pierce the core of me,
small arrows tipped with my own blood.

They accuse me of selfishness.
But you are almost in heaven, I howl,
what could *I* possibly give you?
Hurling words across the galaxy
that separates the living
from the not-yet-born, I explain
galaxy comes from *gala*,
in Greek it means milk.
There is, I insist, sustenance
in the starlight around you.

But they will not have it.
They do not
believe in new-age crap
or etymology, they want
flesh and breath.
They want me.
Little demons.
I know these children
are mine.
They demand the bloody earth.
Heaven does not interest them.

The Last Shelter

The Speed of Rust

It rains.
My heart disintegrates for other reasons
while the bald eagle gazes at me
from the lifeguard's chair.
His head is not white but scuffed, dirty.
He may look like a bird of prey but in fact
he is a fifty-two-year-old man
who has just crawled out of bed
with a hangover and a wife
he rarely loved well.

Whatever
was fine weather
in his life has turned
to the swamp-sky of March,
rain in April, through June,
and tomorrow is the first of July
though it's hard to consider
celebrating Canada Day
with anything but a scream.

Which the bald eagle does:
the serrated thrust of his voice
shreds the grey light as he opens
his wings and lifts, lifts,
heaves himself into the heavy air.
There he goes, flapping over our stunned heads
toward the jungle that stalks Vancouver
like a panther, the same jungle
I fought in cold blood this morning,
so much fierce bamboo.

You and I walk the wide sand flats,
slick pewter acres of seaweed,
cracked shells, crabs scuttling sideways
like our desire. We are so close
to the barges that we see
a modern galley slave moving
feverishly about on the long deck.
He is silent in labour, I am silent
in sympathy, listening to you tell
how you think maybe you can't marry her.

I suddenly remember my hedge clippers
lying on the grass in the back garden.
Tools rust if you leave them out
in this rain. They teach us, every year,
not to do it again.

Why it's all wrong takes so long to explain
that the tide begins to embrace our cold feet.
You could save yourself by drowning
but do not: we walk back to the stony shore
littered with condoms and weddings,
one of which will take place in exactly
forty days. You ask, a tear in your eye,
How much longer will it rain?

I reply, You're lucky enough
to have choices. Old lover,
surprise yourself and make one.
Useless advice, like all advice
must be at this moment. You wring
your heart on the beach while on the far shore
landmines explode, men labour on
prison ships, children drown in wet sand
similar in weight to this wet sand
but lethal, marbled with blood,
impossible to walk away from.

You say you cannot walk away.
I say *I know, I know,* and think again
of my clippers in the grass,
the speed of rust. I say,
You are a good man
and she is a good woman.

Kissing you goodbye, I wonder if
that is how bad marriages are made:
the hungry shovel of the heart
wants to break the clean surface of goodness,
get to the rich filth underneath.

I like how mistakes wait in our hands
like the orchids we crave for their beauty.
And because we don't know how to grow them.
I like that we want to learn.
I love how we fail.

Swimming Lessons on Vancouver Island

i.

Another spring cracks open
              as the seagull drops living mussels on stone shore.

              I know the fierce gull.
              I know the creature
              torn from its shell.

ii.

The sea laps, licks,
              seizes the stone foot of the house,
    sea like a beast,
    sea like a beast I know.
When I was a child, it held me down.
The one who went before,
              my mermaid sister,
                drowned.
    Yet I have learned to love

              water: the ocean beyond measure,
                every sea, the river of my birth,
             the lake that pulled me under
                into memory.
             Finally we love the beast
                that lets us go.

iii.

Red tulips burn the edge of the bay, rock cress cascades
        purple and white
            daffodils cry yellow
                bobbing idiots   sun-stunned
            I can't understand it   can't understand
                the foreign beauty   so gaudy
                            nothing
                            is real here
                            I am not real
                my head floats past my feet
                            I cannot retrieve it.

iv.

Oh Canada.
        I try so hard with you
        but nothing explains
        your ferocious polite immensity,
                your merciless wind, your deaths,
                    which are my own.
                Not to suggest that a country
                    is a family

                but stating it unequivocally
                a country *is* a family
                    and this is mine,
                    my country,
                    my family.

It is the dead
        who teach us how to live,
well or badly, it is the dead
        who teach us how to swim,
well or badly, it is the dead
        who walk among us
                but cannot spell our names.

v.

The otter does not speak human.
The heron neither.
Oh, smiling seal,
      brown-eyed siren, could you be
           my brother?
           my sister?

I regard the green water
      as longingly
      as it regards me

         yet I no longer understand
           what animal I am,
           what is my language.

Oh, country of rock and salt,
      vault of drowned jade—

         open your doors.

If I do not find the truth
      on my own cold shore
         then I cannot swim well
         through the world.

River Sister

For Jennifer

i.

Winter's end, she had to sell the Bronco.
She slept on the riverbank
through the spring
hidden by wolf willow,
scrub balsam, old tarpaulin.

Sleeping by the river, she said.
In poetry, that's romantic
        but for me it was more
          rheumatic.
And she laughed.

But looked sick. No fat left anywhere,
even her butt and breasts smoked off.
Skeletal. Yet young.
A child's eyes
sent up smoke signals
from the burnt sockets
in her skull.
I tried not to look
at the sores on her neck.

She could not sit still.
We walked the path along the Bow
through the empty Stampede grounds
and back again.

Early summer, horse-smells
behind the track
and a rope of scent coming off her,
cigarette smoke,
perfume, sweat.

Behind us
beside us
the river
the river.

A small story she told:
>Once I woke before dawn and heard some guy singing.
>Not in English, his own language.
>I knew he was singing to the river.
>He was like the river turned human.
>Made me shiver. I was freezing my ass off out there
>so I was always shivering, but you know what I mean.
>Shoulda been scared shitless
>because I was alone and those guys
>can be dangerous but somehow I knew
>he wouldn't hurt me. And he didn't.

We turned back toward Eighth Avenue.
She wanted to buy sandwiches for the girls,
coffee to dull the scythe of downtown wind.
I paid, happy for it, something.
But she would not eat with me.

ii.

When I return to Calgary
I walk to the Bow alone,
touch my hands to the water.
My great grandfather walked
these riverbanks with my mother
when she was five years old
skinny girl in pig-tails
racing up the bank
to greet the lions
on the Centre Street Bridge.

They coughed up candies
when he tapped the beasts
with his cane.

My grandmother swam
in the deep eddies upstream.
I swam here, too, as a girl,
and farther, colder away,
Bragg Creek, Banff, in between
where the water slides glacial green,
sings *a capella* of ice and clasps the heart
of any warm body tossed in the rapids,
colours the eyes cobalt aquamarine flashed silver oh
the fishness of this river! The trout
I knew writhing ahead of me as I stroked
into the current, head aching, flesh chilled
and shivering for hours after I came
dripping out of it, walked onto the island,
met an owl in a tree
and smiled at the mousebone
show of skat below her royal owlness.

I canoed the Bow hard
wishing it might carry me
to the far sea I craved.
But every trip ends in Calgary.

Prince's Island. Sunnyside. River
as city, river as the story I know.
Azure on a sunny day but always
clear and cold up close
the empty colour of the tissue
that covers the eye
transparent
though so much filth rushes through.

I stumble down to the water
plunge my hands into the cold blood
of our common mountains.
I do not sing
I do not know the river words
but I watch the rushing oracle
and ask

       Where is she?

       River sister
       where have you gone?

Animal Life

For Mara

The thermometer reads -23° Celsius.
It's colder in the wind-raked field
where she is
trying to convince Dog Meat
he has nothing to fear.

Dog meat no longer. Lucky gelding.
She rescued him at auction.
After he spooks, she high-steps
through the snow again.
Three hours plus five acres yields
two holy ghosts, white breath rising.

He grabs a mouthful of oats from the bucket,
jerks his head away. Inside the dirty gloves
her fingers ache with cold

as they ached years ago
when the chickens' feet
were freezing on the farm,
turning the grey that burns
to frost-bite black.
She was seven and sobbing,
poppy-cheeked, holding one bird
after another in her filthy coat.
Their beaks were already frozen.

Crouched in the coop, head back,
she howled like one of the children
she used to read about in the tabloids
of her life *Girl raised by wolves!*

The truth is stray dogs
raised her. Traipsing down
the shimmering roads of August,
she disappeared with the mutts and hounds
of the neighbourhood for hours at a time, dawn to dusk,
gone wherever the pack would run her.

Sometimes she came home half-naked,
shoeless, but never stolen,
saved by the beasts who brought her back
day after day.

Two decades later,
the bay gelding sidles,
drags a hoof through
the crusty drift,
bares his teeth.

Her coaxing voice unmoors him.
He knew boots before,
a stick with a nail in it.
Why don't you just leave me alone?

But the woman is resolute
as a wolf. Or a grinning stray.
She stalks her prey
patiently through the snow
toward the warm green mouth
of spring.

Possession

The door opens—she
The door bangs against the wall—she cannot
The door slams shut—she cannot remember

how she got this far
She stumbles down the steps
in a t-shirt, nothing else
blood footprints behind her
She got out

But where are her shoes?

She wouldn't let him
Not now
Her clothes are in the house
Stop it
Her washing machine photographs cutlery
are in the house also

She screamed *Get off me*
He swore
hoisted himself up
She thought it was done

but when he turned around he had
the base of (her) standing lamp in his hands
He swung it around, around, the cord
whipping a medieval song through the air

then he let it fly
she dropped to the floor
the lamp hit the mirror
The unexpectedly
metallic shattering
offered her one undivided thought

If I do not get out of my house now
I will die in it.

* * *

She says to herself:
He thinks I am a shovel.
He will pick me up
and dig into his own hard flesh,
the clay of the soldier, the clay
of death.

If he digs himself out
will he bury the rest?

I am a tool.
Use me. Use me.

Where did those words
come from? She wonders
if she learned them
before she could talk.

He's gone away.
She returns, sits alone
in the kitchen. No food
in the fridge, the house
a demolition site
again.

Still, she is pleased to feel
her own hunger.

In the silence, the question
When will he come back?
floats like an apparition
above the stove.

It might be the ghost
of her mother
or the insomniac spirit
of a woman who lived here once.

Maybe it's her.
Maybe she is the ghost.

* * *

She writes a grocery list
          apples
          tomatoes
          almonds
          bread
          cheese

It always comes down to this,
her two hands, a cigarette, a piece
of paper scrawled with bald need.

I am a spoon, she says to herself.
Hold, stir me.
I am a red bowl.
But writes, under *bread*:
knife.

Then she raises her head.
What's that phrase?
Someone walked over
my grave.

He is home now.
He is walking
up the front steps.

Group Portrait by Starlight

Cochrane, Alberta

I lie in the cabin
under a spiral of stars.
I have plans to talk with my family.
The ones who have shown up.
The younger brother is in jail,
the youngest sister is still missing.
The others are stretched out
on the floor beside me
on a couple of cots.
We are listening to the river.

Why are you awake? asks one voice.
At first I think it's my mother.
Then I realize it's my older sister,
her voice grown deeper in death,
smokier. (Yes, they have
du Mauriers in heaven.)

I answer, I am awake because you are.
I'm thinking about you.

Lying right next to me is the child.
He is the son of the missing woman,
little river sister.

He is six years old.
His name means *light*.
I try to explain
that his mother
is sick, she cannot
come to save him.
Neither can I.

Why not? he asks in his practical voice.

Because I live too far away from the river
where you are drowning.
And the social worker says no.
And I am poor.
And my address is in another country.

He replies, grave and weary
in this night of adult excuses,
            But, Auntie, your address is always
            in another country.

I respond with nothing.
Even silence cannot match his eloquence.
Will he remember us, after they deliver him
to his new family?
The social worker promises
we can write to him.
She promises
we will see him again.
She promises this
will not be the last visit.
No one else will disappear.
Naturally she is lying.

It's glorious out here. Black.
I believe I hear the slow diamond-churn
of stars, the gutted light of the universe
raining down upon us.

Or is it just my stomach growling?

On cue, my mother asks,
            Are you hungry, dear?
Tears spike my eyelids.
Am I *hungry*?

Did she bring food
for everyone, or just for me?

Without giving me
time to reply, she asks another question,
Are you all right?

I'm fine, Mom. Fine.
These small words, like tacks between the teeth,
pressed to the tongue, hold up the entire picture.

My eyes rove the camp beds,
seeking him out. My father.
His profile resolves into itself,
visible against unfinished drywall.
Old-Broken-Nose, Old-Canadian-Club
lifetime member.
The grey hair tufts
over the strong forehead.
His concrete-dust hands
hang limp and gentle
as a cadaver's.

But I know he's not dead
because I can hear him snoring.
The innocent sawing
amazes me.
I want to light a candle
and travel the rough years of his face.

But the only light allowed here
is starlight, which drops in
through three small windows.
Surprising, how the dead
fires illuminate the room.

I can even see the ragged scar
on my older brother's forehead.
Stop that before someone
loses an eye!
But he didn't.

Look at the stars, he breathes,
            his voice a distorted
            echo of the child's voice.

I know the two of them,
giant uncle and injured boy,
are holding hands.

There's so much light up there,
            he says to the child,
            who replies with his usual sagacity,
Even though it's so dark down here.

How can I cling to the dumb refrain
the darkness completes the stars?
How can I not?

I whisper to the little boy,
            Don't be afraid.
A useless thing to say.
And possibly bad advice.
            So I add, Little one,
                        I love you.

I say it again, louder,
because he is fading,
eyes and nose and mouth
separating into petals
of salt and carbon,
rain and light.

They each begin
to dissolve, drift
back toward the stars.

Is that all?

We've hardly spoken.
Please don't leave yet.
Come back.
Come back to me.

Goodbye Auntie.
Sister
Daughter
Goodbye.

Their hands wave
slowly, purposefully,
like hands underwater, stirring,
probing the cold starlit body
of the river.

Shelter on the Banks of the Bow

For Christine Cook

i.

Oh Caaaaaaaa-naa
              daa aaa aaa
My home on native land

That's what we used to sing as kids
ignorant of the arrow's
lethal point.
There's no way to work it out carefully.
You have to tear
through the flesh to get free.
Then there'll be blood
all over the goddamn backseat of the car
again.

It's so good to be back in Calgary,
the brutal downtown streets beside the cold river.
I see they have ripped apart the neighbourhood
where the poor people lived
to make room for well-appointed condos.

I thought my youngest sister
was exaggerating.
I often hope
she exaggerates the bad news
but as usual she was telling the truth.

The bulldozers are silent on Sunday
          sunk in mud
          rotten wood
          tarpaper shingles.

The houses smudged out,
the people erased
        along with their useless history.

What is the use of a people's history?

What is the use of my life, half-spent,
the past
        shed

        empty and dry as snake skin
                behind me.

        Get thee behind me
                memory is a long
                        writhing animal, sinuous container
                                shockingly quick
                                        to strike.

ii.

In school and hating it
I loved a girl named Face who made
masks, amulets, mementos
of bone.

She lived in the attic of an old house
        a slanted room inhabited
        by dead animals feathers books
                Weasel Paw   Bird Skull
                        Owl Claw clasping a
                                whorl of Horse's Black Hair.

Our friendship grew from the pulsing
remains under her hands, their bones
as marrow-filled as our own but free.
Suddenly, twenty five years ago
her masks took shape on the paint-stained floor
then stared at us from the walls
like the wild creatures we wanted to become.

And became.
I witnessed her peculiar craft,
watched her sneak away,
took the measure of the night
without her. Waited.
And woke to find water
boiling for tea
her boots by the bed
the smell of the river cold and wolf-willowy
come into the room like a wolf with her.

We did not care about the broken lock. Fool
hardy I think we wanted it smashed let the doors
swing off their hinges let the wind blow in
with the crazy men let the wind stay. I had seventeen

to her eighteen years, both of us gone
from home early and hungry for usage, scraping
our knees against the world.

World showed through sharper
in those raw streets than in the classrooms,
the five dollar jobs, the orderly downtown kingdom
to the west where we watched men
pound steel and glass into the sky and craved
the perilous industry of it, the metal and power
we would not have a place inside.

That world. Finished. Between the racetrack
and the river. That time of immense inarticulate lusts
while around us men articulated their horniness
just fine copped a feel leaned in close
grabbed a piece of flesh to make sure we grasped
their generosity in not taking it all.

iii.

Face and I lay on the gritty attic floor with scalding tea
talking long Camus lines into the unquiet dark.
Someone was always screaming
in one of the houses.
At night I worried for the children
I watched during the day
flint-faced ancient kids
worn out by six or eight or ten years of storm.
A sullen boy kicked a ball against the chain-link fence
made a sound like aborted lightning
while his sister licked salt out of an empty bag of chips
her bruised wrists poking from dirty sleeves.

Their eyes. Beyond the stone
of accusation, the unhideable call
for alms *Give me*
something
more.

The autumn light unwrapped the world
every morning, untangled from the aspens
led us out of the maze of the house
onto the sagging porch
where men smoked and grew quiet.
Variously wrecked, sometimes black-eyed
from the raucous night before
but quiet now.
Maybe venturing to ask
if we had milk for tea.
One of them a gifted carver.
I was too shy to talk to him but admired
the thickly knotted hands a purple thumb nail
a few tools on the porch rail
grey dust in a ring before him on his clothes his face
as though he had carved himself out of stone
and risen up alive, rough-hewn. Human.

iv.

Everyone on the street knew Agatha
the old lady with withered tea bags
scavenger for butts in the gutter.
Once I brought her a box of Tetleys.
The gratitude almost gave her a heart attack.

How she stank. What a wild sweet rose she was.
A girl still sighed in her swallow's cry:
no throaty cackle for Agatha.

I believe she was still sipping tea in her house
twig scarecrow in a holey sweater
when a bladed machine
ploughed the place down

buried her under mouldy drywall and dolls
newspapers and paper cups, photographs
from the forties, pearl strands
as yellow as her teeth.

When I picked through the mess
and the mud yesterday
I found Face's old street only because
I could hear Agatha screaming

> *Those selfish pricks at City Hall,*
> *they'll never get me out of here!*

v.

Not a door or window left of that time

Nothing to walk back inside
only recollections of people scattered
          nameless or forgotten

What is the use of a people's history?

Two bulldozers
          a backhoe
                    grey sky
                              torn net of snow

          a bum stumbles by, stinking old
          god with bandages on blackened hands

I stand in the frozen mud
wondering
how to enter again

that unlikely tenderness
the cracked ribcage of the world

as if it were the last shelter

No Hunter in the Field

now comes the part
where the father
lies dying

at last

this part has taken
my whole life to arrive
I've waited for it
like a child starved
for Christmas

forgiveness is

the old man
coughing up
the slag in his lungs
his face hollowed out
ashen with the work of it

his fingers are gnarled
but they grip the steering wheel steadily
hold fast against gusts of wind
feints of ice
he knows the road with his body

he drives himself
towards death
wearily, irritated
by the traffic
for chrissake these assholes
never signal

(though after the poem
he will rally. typical.
he will go to white sand,
blue sea, Thailand,
and lie down
with a black-haired woman)

but today I believe he will not survive
the winter. so it's kind of him
to drive me
back to the house
for Christmas dinner
the first one I've been to
in a decade

the animals
will be cooked
before I arrive
nothing has to be gutted
or plucked, thank God

forgiveness is

strange
that the car
smells so strongly of him
cement dust
cigarettes
rye

I thought that the smells
would diminish with him
stranger still is the
anger
absconded

I glance around as we drive
digging to find the old fury
that shakes the body
ruptures mind underskin
throat caving in hammering shut—

but it's cast out of me
no demon between us
no hunter in the field

just blown snow
under herringbone sky
I sit beside an old man
who cannot hurt me

forgiveness is—

what?

a deer no one
has ever tracked

the coyote I glimpsed many times
but could not touch until now

the long spine of grass piercing snow

the ribs of an old fence

the lone grace
                of a tree

                        out there
                        speaking plainly

                        Watch
                        here is a way to stand
                        in the world

and when I push open the door
the ice-splash
of wind in my face
is forgiveness

   wake up, you are alive

this air! this freezing air
floods my nose
my throat

yes! come
cold river
rush in

Acknowledgements

Thank you to the early readers: Linda Griffiths, Ann Shin, Anne Bayin, Diana Fitzgerald Bryden, Judy Wearing, Susan Musgrave, Libby Oughton, Nancy Holmes, Helen Tsiriotakis. There have been other readers and supporters, too, over the decade that I spent working on *Come Cold River*. I am grateful to all, especially to Robert Chang. My siblings put up with everything I write about them without a word of complaint or remonstrance (though they do, of course, make jokes at my expense). They have my profound gratitude and love: Jennifer Kochis, David Connelly, Mara Peterson, Ken Connelly. My mother Jackie Henry did not get a chance to read many of these poems before her death, but her life and her courage informs them all. She was the first person to show me that the Bow River and its wild and citied places was story, mythology, history, home. She has returned to those waters.

I am grateful to every hard-working one at Quattro Books, especially to Allan Briesmaster for his editing acumen. Some of these poems have appeared in slightly altered forms in the following publications: *Alberta Magazine, Echolocation, Exile, Geist, The Literary Review of Canada, The Walrus*, and *TOK*.

I learned a great deal about how the wider political atmosphere of a country influences art institutions while I was trying to find a publisher for this book. Therefore, I would like to thank the publishers and their readers who rejected *Come Cold River* with a variant of these criticisms: "Haven't we all heard these stories before? What new emotion or perspective can we find here regarding the murder and abuse of these women and children?" These are, truly, the critical questions. I will never stop thinking about them.

Other Quattro Poetry Books